FORTNITE

The Ultimate Step By Step Guide To Becoming A Pro In Fortnite Battle Royale | Elite Tips, Tricks and Strategies Of A Real Pro

Table Of Contents

INTRODUCTION

Want to finally be the last one standing in Fortnite: Battle Royale? Great! You've certainly come to the right place. In this book I'll be sharing some of the most amazing pro tips, tricks and strategies that will help you destroy your enemies, build better, survive The Storm and much more.

So whether you're a Fortnite newbie or an avid player, you can easily use my book as a guide to your next big win.

Now, are you ready? Okay, let's jump right in!

WHAT IS FORTNITE: BATTLE ROYALE?

When you hear people talking about Fortnite, they're most likely talking about *Fortnite Battle Royale*. which happens to be the standalone free mode of *Save the World*. In short, this game is a massive online brawl where 100 players jump out of a plane, then land onto a small island where they fight each other until only one person is left.

Hidden around this colorful island are handy weapons and other items, including medkits, grenade launchers, sniper rifles and shotguns that every player must be armed with while they explore the landscape and buildings. Players can even collect resources with their pickaxe to build structures that they can use to hide or defend themselves.

As the match goes on, the playable area of land becomes smaller and smaller thanks to The Storm, forcing the players closer together – so the strategy of hiding until everyone else is killed only works for so long.

After battling it out, the last one standing will be named the winner.

But why is everyone so obsessed with Battle Royale? Well, honestly its super engaging for everyone, even spectators. It has a cool theme, a pretty simple premise and fun characters.

You can also play with other online friends or when you're actually sitting next to each other on the couch. Plus, if (or when) your character bites the dust, you can still watch the player who took you out as they continue through the map.

There's also the adrenaline rush you get while taking out other players and the satisfaction of being the sole survivor among 99 other people once you've won. Most people try to say that winning isn't everything, but we both know that isn't true.

Now, let's get into everything you have to know to be the last man (or woman) standing!

FORTNITE: BATTLE ROYALE TIPS, TRICKS AND STRATEGIES

Beginners' Overview

Okay, before I head into all tips and tricks in this Battle Royale book, I also want to share a quick Beginners guide for, well, any Fortnite newbies who don't know all the ins and outs yet. If this is old news to you – and you're just here for the pro tips, then go ahead and skip to the next section. If you want to quickly get more familiar with everything from the resources you'll need to what weapons to carry, then keep reading.

So here's the lowdown on how Fortnite Battle Royale plays and what it features;

- The game is completely free to play, but you can purchase premium editions of the game that will grant you access to exclusive EXP boosters, cosmetic items and much more.

- Right now, there is just one map you can use, but EPIC hasn't ruled out creating another in the future.

- You can play the game solo, duo or as a group with up to 3 other friends.

- All the players begin with nothing in a flying bus that travels across the map. You get to choose when you parachute out.

- You can gather resources to build structures like defense walls and stairs over steep surfaces. Not all materials are created equal, certain ones are stronger than other so they'll provide longer protection.

- The shrinking Storm Eye will make sure that no one can simply hide away and dodge combat (although people try) by creating a playable field or circle. Anyone who doesn't move into the new play zone will suffer damage and eventually die.

- You're completely on foot during Fortnite since it doesn't have any vehicles.

- Every week the game features Weekly Challenges that players can complete and earn in-game cosmetic rewards.

- Epic often has Limited-Time Game modes that will change up the traditional Battle Royale formula.
- Check out the Item Shop so you can buy new Pickaxes, Outfits and more.

Now onto the guide!

The Opening Stage

From the moment you land, you'll need to keep these three things in mind to increase your chances of surviving.

- During the opening stages of a match, it's vital, I repeat, vital that you try to grab as much loot as possible. At this stage in the game you'll need weapon options, shields, ammunition and building resources, and I mean lots of resources.
- As you're looting your enemies, be careful! Take an extra few seconds to check out your surroundings and make sure you're safe enough to secure that loot.
- When you're just starting out in Fornite: Battle Royale, aim to minimize deaths and forget about maximizing your kill count. Of course, it's good to chase the fights to learn how to play the game, but don't focus all of your energy on your kill-death-ratio.

Weapons to Have

Let's just cut to the chase, the most important items to have in your collection are a Shotgun, Assault Rifle and a Sniper Rifle. These three are the best ways to start your arsenal and will set you up nicely for the rest of the game.

Here are the items you should always try to get your hands on in order of importance.

- Shotgun
- Assault Rifle
- Sniper

- Meds
- Shield

Everything else in Battle Royale is a luxury, and they'll certainly help you win the game, but the items listed above are the core foundation of your winning strategy.

If you want to gain more accuracy while shooting an automatic weapon –well, let's be honest who doesn't, then try burst firing.

Also, I'm just going to add a little note about the highly sought-after and talked about Rocket Launchers here. Even though they're useful to have later on in the game, during the earlier stages of a match it needs to sit further down on your shopping list. So, don't spend too much time searching for it and focus on building your winning foundation.

Quick Weapons and Ammo Tips

- You'll notice weapons and ammo from afar since they glow and float in the air.This also applies when someone bites the dust, so you don't need to check the body to know what loot is up for grabs.
- As you may already know, weapons and resources can come from Treasure Chests inside buildings which you can hear a little before you see them because of their shimmering halo-ish noise. These Treasure Chests often hold rare loot and some resources, so they're definitely worth tracking down. You can look for these Treasure Chests everywhere including different rooms, basements and upstairs – also feel free to knock down a couple of walls to reach them.
- Weapons do work differently in Fortnite than PUBG. There's no separate attachments that are needed, all weapons come fully equipped with scopes and any other modifiers.
- I'll be going over more info about Fortnite's weapons later on in this book.

The Environment, Your Movements and Traps

Your movements as you walk around the island can work with or against you, so here are some things that every beginner should know.

You need to remember when your roaming around the island that it's not wise to run into every building you see. For one, there could be a person inside that knows you are near. And even though they can hear you coming, you can't see their exact location. Now this is definitely a huge disadvantage for you, so DON'T go stalking them through the interior of the building. Instead, wait for them outside and catch them by surprise when they come out.

Your building materials will also come in handy as a clever way to trap your enemies. Just create a structure that wraps around the occupied building. Then you'll be able to stake them out from above without putting yourself in a very vulnerable position.

Now, if you're moving from one building or location to the next, avoid running around in the open whenever possible. You can use the trees, buildings or cliffs to help you from being spotted.

And lastly, remember that headphones are definitely a must! They will allow you to hear when other players are coming towards you. Since the sound of movement is loud, it will give you a clear advantage and allow you to prepare for oncoming enemies.

Building and Resources

It's super important that you keep enough resources on you at all time! You really need to be able to build an emergency wall or shelter whenever it's needed. So ideally, you'll need to always have minimum of around 300 of each resource. Some players opt to carry around 400 -500, so you can do that as well if you wish.

I know it's really easy to get caught up in chasing kills and scoring the strongest weapons, that gathering resources can quickly become an afterthought until later on in the game. But I can't stress how important it is to have these resources available!

You never want to be in a position where you can't build a ramp or a few walls to take cover just because you didn't gather enough supplies.

Just so you know, wood is great for creating quick buildings, while stone and metals are the best for creating lasting late-game forts.

Please note that if you're a PUBG player, you'll need to get used to finally building stairs and quickly get up sloped areas like everyone else. So, don't forget that you can place walls just about anywhere, which is really useful when you're under heavy fire and want to gain the upper hand.

There's also tons of other items you can gather to make different things which I'll get into below.

Get to Know Your Crafting Materials

Like I mentioned before, resources are highly important throughout the course of the game. But a lot of players don't know what goes into crafting everything from traps to weapons and forts, or where to find them. Well, you're not going to be this player!

In this section, I'll tell you exactly what you can build and where to find these crafting materials.

Ore

Ore is basically the material that you need to craft just about any weapon in the game. You will start with all weapon schematics asking for copper ore, then the schematics will evolve to a different kind of ore that will be needed like this - Copper > Silver > Malachite

> Obsidian > Brightcore. After getting up to level 4 (Obsidian), you can then choose between using obsidian ore or creating a crystal weapon.

When you go searching for ore, you need to look for something that looks sort of like a cave with rocky overhangs or in actual cave areas, which will appear on all the maps. You can find bigger caves on the Forest and Grassland maps, but it's easier to find caves on the outskirts of the Suburbs, Cities or Industrial area since they're much smaller and easier to search.

You can find Ore here:

- **Copper** – Located in Stonewood
- **Silver** – Located in Late Stonewood & Plankerton
- **Malachite** – Located in Late Plankerton & Canny Valley
- **Obsidian** – Located in Late Canny Valley & Twine Peaks
- **Brightcore** – Located in Twine Peaks

Mechanical Parts, Nuts and Bolts

In this game you can't make anything work without Mechanical parts. You'll need to use them when crafting just about everything including sniper rifles, assault rifles, explosive weapons, wall lights and ceiling drop traps, just to name a few. Mechanical parts also evolve with your schematics, which means you'll need different kind of parts.

You can occasionally farm up nuts and bolts, and you'll likely get a few mechanical parts too. Also, try looting toolboxes and other crates, but these aren't always great. Many players think that the best place to find nuts and bolts is by destroying a car, but actually the parking meter drops the most.

Here's where you can find different types of Mechanical Parts:

- **Rusty mechanical parts** – Located in Stonewood
- **Simple mechanical parts** – Located in Late Stonewood & Plankerton

- **Sturdy mechanical parts** – Located in Late Plankerton & Canny Valley
- **Sleek mechanical parts** – Located in Late Canny Valley & Twine Peaks
- **Efficient mechanical parts** – Located in Twine Peaks

Mineral Powder

Unlike the other crafting materials, Mineral powder is something you can have way too much of, but still worry about having too little of it because it's an essential part of many schematics. You can use it to craft shotguns, axes, swords, scythes, wall dynamos, freeze pads, wall launchers, ceiling zappers, floor launchers and freeze pads.

Mineral powder is super easy to gather since you can get it when you destroy an ore or a rock. The kind of mineral powder you'll need will also evolve as you evolve schematics.

- **Rough mineral powder** – Located in Stonewood
- **Simple mineral powder** – Located in Plankerton & Late Stonewood
- **Fine-grain mineral powder** – Located in Canny Valley & Late Plankerton
- **Char-black mineral powder** – Located in Twine Peaks & Late Canny Valley
- **Oxidized mineral powder** – Located in Twine Peaks

Twine

It's just string, but you can make tons of stuff with it in Fortnite. You can use it to use wall darts, pistols, several types of melee weapons, wooden wall spikes and ceiling drop traps.

You can gather it by simply destroying trees, bushes, plants and anything else natural. It might also drop alongside or inside planks. Yet, destroying trees is the best way to go about gathering twine.

Like the other materials listed above, twine will evolve as you evolve schematics and you'll need different kinds.

Here's where you can find different types of twine:

- **Stringy twine** - Location in Stonewood
- **Simple twine** - Locations in Plankerton & Late Stonewood
- **Sturdy twine** - Locations in Canny Valley & Late Plankerton
- **Peaky twine** - Locations in Twine Peaks & Late Canny Valley
- **Carved twine** - Location in Twine Peaks

Planks

Planks can be used often to craft many things including shotguns, a wide variety of melee weapons, wall darts, wall launchers, wooden wall and floor spikes, floor launchers and patrol wards.

Planks are practically needed for everything, but the good news is they're super easy to get. For every tree you chop down, there's a chance to drop some planks. You can also get planks by looting lumber piles.

Also, you should know that other wooden structures do drop planks, but the chances are not as high as chopping down trees.

Rough Ore

Rough Ore is one crafting material that many players seem to always have too much of and never run low on. Well, this is mainly because it's easy to get from the stones you destroy. If you are looking for it in particular, you can find it in any cave by looking for rocks that are dark and somewhat flat in shape.

This crafting material is made to use blasting powder, and it's also used to make laser weapons, wall launchers, retractable floor spikes, ceiling zappers and swords.

Flowers

In Battle Royale, flowers are only used to make healing pads. So, there's really no reason to have more than one full stack on you at a time.

They do drop from plants and bushes, but the best way to farm them is to look for actual flowers. Just choose a Suburb map and look for a garden.

Fibrous Herbs

Get ready to craft healing pads, duct tape and ceiling gas traps with fibrous herbs. And since ceiling gas traps are extremely useful, you will probably go through fibrous herbs faster than you realize.

You can gather these fibrous herbs by searching through anything natural like crops, little plants and bushes (located throughout every map) or by looking through refrigerators and kitchens.

Coal

You can ONLY use coal to craft blasting powder. Thankfully a few stacks go a long way, if it doesn't then you can gather coal in some easy to find places.

There are several places you can find coal like in a fireplace, but the best place to gather this crafting materials is in ore-bearing caves. There you'll find coal nodes that look like small black specks and they're totally different from the other nodes.

Batteries

Just like IRL, batteries are used to power up certain weapons. Instead of listing everything you can, simply assume that all energy weapons (like laser swords and rocket hammers) and traps need batteries to be crafted. You'll also need batteries to create energy ammo as well.

Gather all the batteries you need from tech items or by destroying things like appliances including refrigerators, stoves and washers.

Adhesive Resin

You will only need this crafting material to make duct tape. Adhesive resin - you can just think of as sap- is also quite common since it drops from plants, shrubs and trees.

Bacon

Yup, a touch of bacon is all you need to make things like energy cell ammo, healing pads, ceiling gas traps and defender pads. And if you're using a lot of energy weapons, it will become more precious than gold.

To find it, keep a look out for spam cans while you wander around the wilderness. These little cans will yield bacon 100% of the time. You can also find it in other places like refrigerators or in containers in the kitchen area, oh and grossly enough in the toilets. In fact, toilet bacon is really common.

Rotating Gizmo

You'll need to have rotating gizmos whenever you want to craft pistols, sniper rifles, shotguns, assault rifles or all melee weapons that are Rare or Epic in rarity. You won't need them for Uncommon rarity or Legendary rarity weapons.

Rotating gizmos are a bit different from other crafting material since they can't be gathered from one other source. They can drop from chests or toolboxes, but the highest chances of a drop are from destroying garden gnomes.

Active Powercell

These active powercell are practically a step above rotation gizmos and you'll need them to craft pistols, shotguns, assault rifles, sniper rifles and all melee weapons with legendary rarity.

You can find them in the same areas as rotating gizmos, and they'll mainly be in chests, garden gnomes and toolboxes.

Quartz Crystal

Shining Quartz crystals can be used in a variety of ways, mainly when crafting energy-based weapons. They're also used in a few traps like wall light, freeze pads and patrol wards.

You can farm these crystals in caves and they look like an ore node with white pointy spikes. Also, since there are usually tons of quartz nodes, you'll have no problem gathering a lot in a hurry.

Duct Tape and Blasting Powder

As you go over your mission menu inventory, you might notice a crafting panel off to the side that only holds blasting powder and duct tape. You can find these materials while going through chests in the wild, but the best way to get ahold of them is through making them.

Now, if you're making a trap and don't have enough tape or blasting powder the game will automatically craft them for you with the materials you have (if you have them).

What You Can Build

With all the right resources in hand, you can go ahead and create whatever you want. Below, I'll let you know what structures you can build and how they can help you throughout the game.

Panic Walls

Now, let's start off with something simple – panic walls. These can really save your life out there and give you the advantage when a fight suddenly starts.

When these walls are placed down, they'll absorb bullets coming your way. You can also use them right in front of an opponent so it minimizes any damage and fakes them out.

There are other ways you can use them, like when you're being shot at from the back while running across open ground (something you shouldn't do) or when you've encountered an enemy head on.

How to build:

1. Select wood since it's a common, disposable resource.
2. Select the default wall option.
3. Place the walls in front of you or swivel it and place them behind you.

Tip! Wood won't break as easily as brick or metal when you place it first, that's why it's the go-to resource for planting in a hurry.

Panic Ramps

It's easy to see why Panic Ramps are well loved. They're simple, effective, and they'll give you a height advantage when you need it. When you spot an enemy from a distance, all you have to do is build high, take cover and then peek over the edge when you're ready.

But be warned that ramps are easy to destroy, so the advantage is pretty temporary.

How to build:

1. Place down wooden walls to create a wooden box.
2. Stand in the center of it and place a ramp leading upwards.
3. Finish it by placing a wall behind the ramp.

Panic Ramps (Version 2)

Continuing with the building instructions above, this panic ramp is still easy to build and will give you a height advantage on two sides and provide enough protection while your under fire.

These ramps are good to build while you're engaged in a duel with opponent(s) or when you want a structure that will temporarily hold down a position.

How to build:

1. Create a rectangle out of walls.
2. Stand in the center and place ramps leading upwards on both sides.

Panic ramps are easy to expand on, so if the situation changes, just build to match it.

The Funnel

This is basically Panic Ramp Version 3 since it has two different styles. The first one is a very basic structure that will provide you with great cover and a height advantage. The other one expands on this to give you a wider platform so you and your team can scope out the area safely.

1st Building

1. Build a 2 x 2 box.
2. Stand right in the center.
3. Place the pyramid/roof structure in each of the corners.

The finished product should look like a funnel that sucking you up.

2nd Build

1. Build these stairs going outwards from each of these walls.
2. Place the roof structure in between all of the gaps, making the funnel even larger.
3. Select walls.

4. Run along the structure you have built, placing the walls on the outside. (You can certainly do this while you're in the safety of the funnel. You don't have to stand on the outer edge of the ramps.)

Sniper Tower

When you build a sniper tower you can gain some much needed altitude as well as get a birds eye view and sniper enemies from afar.

But with a building this high, you need to have an escape plan ready. I recommend that you build a ramp that leads down from the top, so you can quickly leave if other players decide to attack.

How to build:

1. Create a small box to encase yourself.
2. Stand to one side, jump and then place a ramp that leads upwards.
3. Move to the highest part of the ramp, build walls, jump and then place a ramp leading upwards.
4. Repeat.

Build the tower as high as you like and use it in several ways. You can build it outwards to reach inaccessible areas, or just to have a crazy sky high fortress.

Editing Builds

When you place a structure like a basic wall for example, you can then go ahead and edit it to make it into something new. You can create a doorway or turn a square wall into an archway. Learn how to edit fast and you can outplay all your opponents!

Selecting Your Starting Location

Last but not least, you have to pick the right spot to land. Why? Because your location in Fortnite will determine whether you have an inventory full of weapons and ammo, or end up running around with just a pickaxe until another player takes you out.

I'll let you know where you can land to avoid the latter at all cost. And don't worry, these tips and strategies are beginner-friendly - well, as long as you know how to shoot, so be sure to practice.

1. Drop away from major locations

Okay, so let's just say that ten people land in a town, odds are one person will make it out alive with all the best loot. You can take advantage of this situation by dropping away from the popular location, gearing up and then swing back around to the town to catch the unaware and loaded victor off guard.

If you can get a clean shot without them knowing you're location, then you'll have the upper hand and it won't matter if their weapons are better. Plus, when you kill them, you get all their loot.

2. Drop late if you want peace and quiet

A lot of players don't like waiting around and drop out of the Battle Bus really early. Use this as a major advantage if you want a slow and steady game. Now if you're looking to go after the action, then drop early.

3. Go the distance

When you choose a drop location that's further away from the path of the bus, you'll be met with way less resistance on land. For example, if the bus is going to the left of the map, the locations on the right will be less popular.

Once you jump out the battle bus, pull your parachute early so you can travel further. The map is pretty small so you can reach just about any location.

4. Playing solo? Then head to more secluded spots

If you're alone, you can just head to smaller drop spots. They'll most likely have a chest or two that will be holding about enough gear for only one person, but not enough for a duo or a four-man squad. So when you do play with friends, make sure you go for a larger location.

5. Pay Attention to Your Surroundings

One of the most important things to remember when you drop is to be aware of your surroundings. You'll need to know where you're aiming and where the other players are dropping.

You can do this while you're in the air by turning and looking for parachutes, then making a mental note of where they're landing. The more you know from the air, the better you'll be on the ground.

More Beginner Tips and Tricks

Okay, here are some more beginner tips that will help you survive in Battle Royale.

- Always use the map to plan your route effectively to the safe circle.
- I did mention that there are no vehicles in Fortnite. But you don't need to freak out when the circle starts moving. The island is actually really small in size. So even if the circle is on the other side of the island, you'll have enough time to get there if you plan well.
- When you finally reach the safe circle, DON'T assume that all the other players are there too, some will still be coming in from the outside. You have to remember this or else you could get shot in the back, but you should also use this info to your

advantage. By running in and getting to a safe building that's nearby, you can easily pick off advancing players.

- Weapon and resources are often located in buildings and other structures, they also appear a lot in populated areas. Of course, this doesn't mean that you should run there for the loot because these areas will attract a lot of other players. You definitely need to weigh the risk of getting better loot vs going up against competition. If you're not ready, then build up some confidence by exploring villages as your arsenal grows or ignore most buildings all together.

- In Battle Royale, it's common for players to close the door behind them when they enter a building. This way it looks like no one is in there and you can catch other players by surprise when they come inside. On the other hand, you can keep the door open as a warning to other players, or to pretend that the house was looted and left abandoned.

- Ideally, you want a variety of weapons for different scenarios - rifles for mid-range fights, sniper rifles for when you're at a distance and shotguns for up-close use.

- Healing items are really rare, but a bandage or med-kit are perfect to have as backup after a few scrapes.

- Crouching is a great way to help hide your presence as much as possible. You can move even faster while crouching by hitting sprint just like you would if you were standing upright.

- Bullets actually leave tracers in Fortnite so you'll be able to tell what directions enemies are firing from.

- If you come across a pile of tires, walk on top of them to spring really high into the air. You can do this if you need to get on top of a building's roof for a better vantage point or when you're being chased and need to lose another player quick.

Lingo to Know

All games have their own kind of lingo and *Fortnite: Battle Royale* is no exception! When you're playing with the squad and your all building bases, sharing loot, calling out the enemy's location or taking them down, communication is key.

And it's no secret that the team with the best communication are more likely to be around in the end. Here are a few basic terms that aren't obvious when you're just starting, but definitely need to learn.

10. BUSH CAMPERS

It means just that – bush campers (people camping in the bushes). It's pretty obvious to seasoned players, but beginners might think there's more depth to it.

9. KNOCK(ED)

Knocking an opponent means you knock an opponent down but you don't fully eliminate them. When you tell a team mate that you've knocked a player, you're letting them know he wasn't eliminated instantly so his teammates are probably still nearby.

Also, letting your teammates know how many players were knocked from an enemy squad will tell you if you guys can rush a shorthanded team or not.

8. LAUNCH(ING)

Launching simply refers to players that are using a launch pad. Saying this will instantly tell your teammates that someone has launched so they need to look up at the sky for diving opponents.

Also, players who with a launch pad can use it as a way to dive in to the next bubble if it happen to be too far away, or towards enemies you want to rush.

It can really help decide your next move when you let your teammates know you have a launch pad.

7. MATS

Mats is slang for materials, which just means things like wood, brick and metal. Your teammates might come to you and ask if you want to share mats or "how are you on mats?" They're referring to your levels of wood, metals and brick(stone).

6. MINIS

A "mini" is sometimes used to refer to mini shields or miniguns, but it's more commonly used to refer to mini shields. Players are only allowed to use 2 mini shields in order to generate a maximum of 50% to their shield gauge.

That's why sharing minis among teammates is really common. Let your teammate know you have a "mini" so you can share a shield potion with them.

5. SHIELD POP

Calling out a "shield pop" to your teammates means you've successfully destroyed an opponent's shield partially or fully.

This will tell your teammates how weak an opponent is, along with how good their weapons and inventory might be. So, when you shoot an opponent's shield and notice that it was full to begin with, this will tell you they likely have some good guns too.

4. ONE-SHOT

"One-shot" is an important phase to remember. When you tell your team an opponent you're looking at is "one shot", it means that opponent is just one shot away from being knocked down completely. This is important because it will let your teammates know whether they should rush an opponent or not.

3. STORM TROOPERS

Nope, this doesn't have anything to do with Star Wars. In Fortnite "Storm Troopers" is a term that refers to opponents who are still within the storm or coming out of the storm.

This is a harsh term used to teased players who are hiding in the storm because they're too scared to face the other players head-on.

2. THE BUBBLE

"The Bubble" is a term that refers to the storm or the force field that determines the playing area. Players normally tell their teammates to "start moving towards the bubble," or "let's build in the final bubble".

And when I say final bubble, that means the last bubble before the playing area disappears entirely.

1. HEALS

When you hear a teammate asking"do you have any heals?" They're asking you if you have any healing items that will increase their health points, not shield. So, anything like bandages, med-kits, chug-jugs, a campfire or slurp potions will help them out. Share your heals with your teammates and you guys can continue on to victory!

Now this is the end of my beginner guide to Fortnite: Battle Royale. So, you'll have no problem understanding everything I'll be getting into next.

ESSENTIAL TIPS, TRICKS AND STRATEGIES

Fortnite: Battle Royale is an easy game for anyone to play, but winning a match isn't something you can achieve without playing well. There are things you have to know and avoid to be the last one standing. With that being said, in the next few chapters I'll go over all the tips, tricks and strategies that will help you play like a pro, survive to the end and finally win!

Fortnite: Battle Royale – Map Guide

Before I go on talking about the map, you should know that Epic Games does update it every season. The map that I will be going over below is the most updated version for season 4 and it will most likely be changed a bit for the next season. So, I'll give you the lowdown on this new season, along with some timeless tips that will help you out regardless of how much the landscape changes.

New Areas

For Season 4 the landscape has changed a bit thanks to a huge meteor strike. Below, are some of the areas you can explore for loot and shoot it out with your enemies.

Dusty Divot

Once you launch the game, you'll notice just how much the meteor shower changed the map. One of the most noticable changes is to Dusty Depot which is now Dusty Divot. The area is filled with Hop Rocks that will give you a temporary zero-gravity effect.

There's also a cool research center in the middle of the crater that is filled with small tunnels and ramparts that you can fight in.

Risky Reels

Move on toward the North Easternmost point of the map and you'll see a new location named Risky Reels. It used to be a little drive-thru theater, but now it has a huge crater in the middle of it that's surrounded by a few burned out cars.

The Prison

It's not really a new location, but the Prison by Moisty Mire has also been struck by a meteor. Some buildings are completely gone, while others suffered some major damage. I can tell you one things for sure, this area will definitely see some interesting, out in the open fights during the game.

The Best Locations to Loot

Who doesn't want to find some amazing loot? In this section I'll give you a clear idea of where treasure chests are hiding and how much loot you're likely to walk away with! Of course, I promise to be as descriptive as possible to help you easily find them.

The Motel to the West of Anarchy Acres

In this secluded spot you'll see about 5 chest, including two that are out in the open – one inside a truck, while the other one is on a different vehicle's roof.

You can safely get to the rest by landing on the motel's roof before you smash your way inside. Keep your eyes open for enemies and your ears open for loot. This area has enough loot that you can bring your whole squad there.

Once you're done, head on over to Pleasant Park or Anarchy Acres and start looking to make some kills.

The Trucks Southeast of Fatal Fields

This is one of the best places to loot chests without too much competition. At the blue marker you will find a truck that often has a chest, along with a separate weapon – on several occasions I have picked up a few legendary guns.

After you loot that area, head to the broken-down house that is directly southeast from your located. It's pretty easy to see on the map because it sits on a patch of grass that is brighter that its surrounding area.

You might run into another player there, but they most likely won't be expecting you. So, grab that loot and head directly west where you'll soon come across two trucks. The taller one will have two chests and the smaller one sometimes has a chest on top of it.

Once you're all geared up, head towards the circle if its' too far away and get there with your skates. If it isn't, then go north to check out the new film studio in Moisty Mire which has a pretty decent amount of loot (and plenty of other curious players, so be careful).

If nothing is left there, then head over to Fatal Fields and take out anyone who is trying to leave.

Tomato Town (Overlook)

Tomato Town is a pretty decent place to land, but I recommend staying away from the main fight. Head down south of the town, at the blue marker, there you'll see a metal bunker with a staircase that leads down inside the hill with a tunnel that exits out of town. At the staircase you can normally find two or three weapons and at the bottom you might get your hands on a chest.

I'll warn you to be careful here because this is quite a popular spot. You should also know that you can get there by coming in from above and that doing so will give you the drop on anyone that has landed directly in the tunnel, so just listen in all directions for any footsteps.

After you take care of any lurkers, go inside the tunnel and smash down the fake wall which is located on the opposite side of the staircase and left to the blue car. Behind it there should be a hidden chest.

The best part about this spot is that once you're done you can just head back up stairs and onto the hill, which will give you an amazing view of Tomato Town. From there you can watch all the other players who are leaving, ambush them and take their loot.

The Compound North East of Flush Factory

To get to this location you'll need to drop directly on the southeast corner of the compound that will be marked by a tall chimney that sometimes has a treasure chest on top of it. It's important to note that if you grab it, you'll be the first one in the area to have a weapon and you can then take out nearby enemies.

From there, you can loot the large building under the chimney. As you explore the house, look inside the metal container and upstairs for treasure chests. You might get lucky and find two. While your inside, listen for footsteps since this area is pretty active.

The trucks and containers outside between the buildings might have a few chests, while the buildings will normally have one each.

Oh, and there was a new warehouse club added to this area. It is a decent landing place to get a few chests in the rafters but be warned that the music here will drown out any noise from other players and it's also a bit dim.

If you decide to go this route and succeed, you'll really be set up for a while. Also, this is a good place to go to with a partner or squad if you like to avoid named locations.

The Large Tree to the Northwest of the Wailing Woods

In this location you're pretty much guaranteed at least a chest or two, along with a good spot on the map. Although I only recommend heading to this spot if you're playing solo.

Simply aim for the large tree, and while you're dropping there take a look at the high ground over to the south and you should see a weapon on the ground. Grab it and then head over to the truck. The tree usually has about one chest or two chests if you're lucky.

From there, you can either head to Tomato Town where you'll be on a higher ground overlooking most of the buildings, so you'll also be at an advantage. Or you can head directly northeast where you'll find two houses, and one has a basement.

If you're brave enough, head over to the new Risky Reels that is located north of the tree. You can clean up there and then you'll be well armed.

The Tower at the Far Northeast of the Map

This is an old favorite that is worth looking into again after the map's update. The tower is located in the far northeast corner and it can have at least three chests. If you look to the west there's an ice cream truck that usually has two chests. The first chest is located on the top of the tower to the right, so land on the roof if you happen to see a yellow glow through the woods.

Sometimes there's a chest on the west side of the tower, so if you see it be sure to grab it for some guaranteed loot. This area used to be popular during Season 3, but now there's rarely anyone there unless the bus passes over it.

When you're done in this area, run directly west to the abandoned ice cream truck for a chance to loot a couple more chests. Then, head west and clear out those buildings.

The Mountain to The North of Salty Springs

This really isn't really the best looting location for beginners will bad aim. You'll likely get into a few fights since this area is located right in the center of the map.

Just try to make it to the peak of the mountain before anyone else and you'll walk away with two or three hidden chests.

Before you land, get a look at the hill from all angles if you can to locate all the chests. You will have company, so you'll need to think quick if you want to come away with the best weapons.

When you're done there, head over to Salty Springs. Dusty Divot is a bit dangerous because you'll be exposed as you make your way down the crater, so be sure to fill your bag with hop rocks if you go that route.

The Houses That Are West of Shifty Shafts

Although it can be a bit busy, dropping by Shifty Shafts isn't such a bad idea. Sometimes it isn't as busy as other named areas, so just be sure to look for weapons as you glide in and go for the best one.

In my opinion its best to start at the houses located to the west of the main mine shafts. Normally, at least two of them will have one or two chests, along with weapons and ammo.

A lot of players don't know that there are chests located at Shifty Shafts, so even if people are wondering around and shooting it out, you can still sneak over there and nab one or two chests.

Simply stay above ground and keep your ears open.

Compound southeast of Junk Junction

This spot is a great place for duos to drop. The area consists of a cluster of old buildings that most players leave alone, but if you head there you can find three to four chests. Spot it from the sky and land there, because from the ground you can only get the loot by building.

On the way down, look over and see if anyone has landed near Junk Junction and Pleasant Park. If you are lucky with the loot you get, decide whether you should take them by surprise or not.

The Football Field West of Tilted Towers

Tilted Towers is a fun location to drop, but it can be crazy at times. A good way to get around this is to head a little further west, there you'll find a cluster of buildings, and one even has an indoor football field.

That field happens to be the best place to start. There are guns on the pitch, and chances to loot chests on either side of the arena. Once you're done there, head west to the next building which also has some chests to loot.

If you've got some good gear then head back to Tilted Towers and just hope that most of the people have gone. If you want to continue on with a low profile, head northeast towards Loot Lake.

I know this list is quite long, but it should provide you with a great start.

Winning Map Strategies

Now that you know more about the map and loot locations, here are two winning map strategies that anyone can try in Fortnite: Battle Royale.

The first one is a Big Kill strategy, which involves playing around the edge of the map, waiting for the other players, rotating with the circle and killing enemies as they run towards the next playable area. It does take some skill (so practice) and a bit of luck to pull off this strategy, but it's definitely doable.

Besides that, there is a more reliable strategy that will have you immediately rushing to the center of each new circle, and from there you'll need to stay ahead of all the other players. Once you're in position, you need to taking advantage of everything you know about the surrounding terrain and start planning out your vantage points.

This strategy will ensure that you avoid arriving into the new circle at a really bad angle. By bad angle, I mean one where another savvy player can just take you out of the game.

When you rush to the new center, you'll get to check out the entire playing field and quickly take note of good spots and bad spots. Once you decide on the best spot, you'll have plenty of time to set up base before the other players show up.

In terms of what a "good spot" is, I should tell you that higher ground is always your friend. It will give you a great advantage point and it's hard for any enemies below to retaliate against you. You can even use higher ground as a way to sniper from afar and spy.

You can get to these high, sharp slopes really quickly by crafting your way up when you need to get away or want to establish a great camping position.

Just remember to listen closely to your surroundings while you travel through the map. Battle Royal offers tons of visual and audio cues that will help you gain crucial info about where someone is, or if someone is walking nearby. You can make sure they don't hear you by crouching which will muffle your footsteps.

Tips for Using Fortnite's Building Tools

Battling it out with other opponents is easy enough for any player who has ever touched a PC shooter in their life. But when it gets down to the last 10 players in a Battle Royale, that's when things get difficult. During this time the game will completely change, and it will all come down to having perfect aim, fast reflexes and your ability to build an amazing fort within seconds.

For anyone who is new to game, getting the hang of building can be quite a frustrating ability to master. That's why I have a few tips for you below that will help you understand and use Fortnite's confusing building tool.

Gather Resources on The Go

If you don't suspect there's another player nearby, then feel free to keep your pickaxe in hand as you walk or run around. Use it to take swipes at any objects including rocks and cars, and if you're not pressed for time stock up on wood.

You can destroy trees too, but don't finish chopping them down – a disappearing tree will only alert others of your exact location. Also, be sure to stay mobile while you swing the hammer. Squirm while you swing it or jump on a few occasions just to make sure your head doesn't stay still for more than a second. You never know if a sniper might be watching you from a distance.

Use Ramps as Cover in Open Areas

If you really have to make it across an open area and you suspect you're being watched, there's only one thing you can do – get your ramps ready! Zig-zag, jump and build up an occasional ramp as you make your way across. If bullet start flying your way, then start laying down ramps as you run. Keep on sprinting, but don't run up all the ramps you build. They're meant to use partially as cover and to also trick your pursuer into thinking you're about to leap over all the ramps made - but you're not.

So make sure you're behaving erratically, running up random ramps, throwing out a few as distractions at a variety of length and you should make it out alright.

Learn How to Build a Basic Recon Fort

Oh, the basic recon fort. How essential you are in Fortnite, especially for beginners. Whether you need to hold your ground or you're doing a little recon, this little fort will keep you safe on all sides while giving you a way to peek out and take shots at other players.

Build it by dropping four walls around you and then jump up to make a ramp under your feet. If you ever need a better vantage point, you can just build up. And this can be done by placing four walls around the tips of your existing structure, jump up, place a floor underneath you, and then jump up again to create another ramp.

Tip! Don't check out the same spot over and over again. Keep moving and have those voyeures out there wondering where you'll end up next.

Add a Campfire for a Powerful Recon

Now if you happen to get hurt, build a recon fort as a quick defensive and remember that you can also heal yourself while you're shooting it out with a campfire. The campfire can heal you from underneath the ramp in a recon fort. So, drop one when you're out hurting, but still want to keep watch.

Build to Break Your Fall

When you make your floor piece, keep it something that is easy to reach for and you can completely avoid an embarrassing falling death by dropping panels below your feet. As you look down steep inclines and then slide down, you can drop pieces here and there to catch yourself. You'll also need to get a general idea of what kind of fall will do a lot of damage. Be careful when you choose to build and don't go too overboard. Those resources will certainly come in handy later on.

Build Ramp Tunnels to Get you Higher, Safely

It's just a fact that higher ground will always win the most games in Fortnite. But, actually getting there can be a huge challenge if your being shot at. So, when you're in trouble, but need to get up there, just make ramp tunnels.

You can do this by dropping a wall that will serve as the base (a fragile one) for the rest of the structure. From the base, start throwing down ramps to run on – now here's the most challenging part - continue to build a ramp roof from the wall base simultaneously. Doing so will keep you covered from other players who are already higher off the ground.

You will need to go back and forth between the floor and ceiling, but once you get the hang of it (and no one decides to destroy your base), you should be just fine... maybe...

Edit Your Way Out of Any Mess

During those one-on-one building battles, players just build without much thought, resulting in huge towers that go nowhere or forts with like three rows of walls. By all means, resist the urge to destroy your structures if you happen to build yourself into a corner. Instead, look to your enemy and see what editing structures does to them.

When you remove a space from a wall, it will create a window or the perfect opportunity to take a shot at an unsuspecting player. Now if you throw in a back door to your recon fort by removing two blocks (the center middle row and the center bottom row) it makes for a great getaway.

You can also make a hole in the floor of your recon fort and drop through it to achieve the ultimate surprise attack or remove the floor below a camper to completely ruin your enemies day. Or you can try to make a small window that is at least big enough for a remote-control RPG to fly through.

And don't waste your time trying to edit another players' structure(s), you can only make these changes to your own building(s).

How to Build a Pro Fort Quickly

As you start using whatever materials you can find, its essential that you learn how to build quickly. Why? Because you're building speed will definitely give you a better chance of survival in a duel other than aiming and shooting your enemies.

Thankfully learning how to build quickly is super easy to grasp, so I've put together a little guide that outlines all the controls for any platform you happen to have Fortnite: Battle Royale installed on.

On Your XBox One

- **[B]** Toggles the open building menu.
- **Holding [B]** Hold the button to circle to edit a structure.
- **[Y]** Press this button to go through the building menu.
- **[X]** Tap this when you want to pick a trap, tap and hold to interact, or simply hold it to quickly jump to your trap inventory.
- **[LB]** Change the building material.
- **[LT]** Equip your targeted building piece.
- **[RB]** Press this to rotate the structure.
- **[RT]** Press this to place a structure.
- **[Right Stick]**: Reset your building edit.

On Your PS4

- **[Circle]** Toggles the building menu.
- **Hold [Circle]** Hold the circle to edit any structure.
- **[Triangle]** Press this to go through the building menu.
- **[Square]** Tap this when you want to pick a trap, tap and hold to interact, or simply hold it to quickly jump to your trap inventory.
- **[R1]** Rotate a structure.
- **[R2]** Place a structure.
- **[L1]** Change the building material.
- **[L2]** Equip your targeted building piece.
- **[Right Stick]** Reset your building edit.

On Your PC

- **Q**: Will instantly bring you to the building menu and defaults to build walls.
- **F1, F2, F3, F4**: You can click on these to go through your building options (example: platforms, ramps etc.)

- **F5**: Press this to place traps on any flat surface.
- **RMB**: Just right click to view all the materials you're using.
- **G**: Press when you want to edit an existing structure. You can add extra doors, create ledges and much more.
- **R**: To rotate a structure.

Rebinds to Build Faster

Now that you know the controls, you definitely need to rebind your control scheme to build and create much faster.

These rebind options for walls, ramps and flat platform happen to be the best so far:

- Building option 1 (wall): Q or E
- Building option 2 (platforms): F or V
- Building option 3 (ramp): F or V

You can also try setting up the building options like this:

- Building option 1 (wall): Z
- Building option 2 (platforms): X
- Building option 3 (ramp): C

And here are a few tips and tricks that will help you build a little bit faster and better.

- Playing on your PC? Then make sure your general mouse sensitivity is set up just right from the start. If it's too low, then you'll find a much harder to swing around in a circle and quickly build around yourself. You'll need to take some time to play with the settings to find a nice, comfortable balance between speed and accuracy. It will definitely help with your building skills.
- Since the contracting circle is constantly moving and shifting, it would be really foolish to start building early on in the game. Instead, you'll need to wait until the

final few phases – when the final playing field is obvious, and you are waiting for players to come to you- then it will be totally okay to start building during this time.

- Combat Pro Control are optional controls that are on PS4 and Xbox One. They allow players to change the default control scheme to something different. So even though building on a console is far trickier than PC, many players swear by the Combat Pro settings. Players say it helps them build faster since it allows them to instantly swap weapons and select building pieces.

- I know I'll say it throughout this book, but you need to practice! For a few games just forget about winning the matches, and completely focus on getting familiar with the controls and improving your building skill. For example, you can try building for the sake of gaining an advantage or to protect yourself.

Everything You Need To Know About Fortnite Healing & Shields

While you're battling it out and having fun in Fortnite, you're bound to get a couple of wounds. In this section I'll go over everything you need to know to recover from any damage and get back in the game.

Below you'll find the basic info you need to know about healing and shields in Fortnite: Battle Royale all in order from weakest to strongest!

The BASICS

Bandages

Bandages will only help you heal up to a maximum of 75 hp when you use them. These are usually the first thing to go in your loadout, unless you want to have multiple healing options while you play.

- Bandages drop in stacks of 5
- Maximum stack is 15

- A bandage will take 4 seconds to use
- Each bandage heals for 15 hp
- You can only heal to 75 hp with bandages

Med Kit

Med kits are awesome since they can heal to full 100% hp. Their only drawback is that they take a bit of time to use. So honestly, they aren't recommended if you need to be healed quick or you're out in the open.

- Drops 1 at a time
- Maximum stack is 3
- A med kit takes 10 seconds to use
- Each med kit heals you for 100% of your hp

Cozy Campfire

Campfires are a bit different than the other healing options on this list. For starters, you can find it in the traps section, it has to be placed on the ground and it can heal both you and your teammates when you guys get near it.

If your health is really low, then you can place two campfires on the ground and stand in between them and get ready to heal quicker.

- Drops 1 at a time
- As far as I know, it stacks in your trap inventory so there's no maximum
- You place it on the ground/floor.
- Campfires can heal for 50 hp.
- Campfires ticks for 2 hp per second for 25 seconds.
- Can heals anyone who comes near it, including enemies!

Slurp Juice

Slurp juice works to kind of heals and kind of protects you. Once you drink it will give you 25 hp and provide a shield for over 25 seconds - pretty much ticking for 1 point of hp and shield every second.

You should know that you can only have one slurp juice at a time, so if you have two you'll have to finish the first one before you can have another. Use these for when you need to top your health after using bandages and are maxed out at 75 hp.

- Drops 1 at a time
- Maximum stack is 2
- Slurp juice takes just 2 seconds to use
- Each slurp juice will heal you for 25 hp and give you 25 hp in 25 seconds along with a shield
- Provides 1 health & 1 shield for each Slurp juice

Small Shield Potion

A small shield potion will give you 25 shields each. You should also know that you can't use them above 50 shields. But they are very fast to use and great in the middle of a battle. Drink it before anything else, so you get to the max of 50 hp with these small shield potions before you start drinking some slurp juice or a bigger shield potion.

- Drops in stacks of 3
- Maximum stack is 10
- A small shield potion will take 2 seconds to use
- Each one of these small shield potions will give you 25 shields
- You can't go above 50 shields with these

Shield Potion

This particular shield is much slower than the small version, but on the plus side it will get you up to the maximum of 100 shields.

- Drops in a stack of 1
- Maximum stack is 2
- A shield potion takes just 5 seconds to use
- Each shield potion gives you 50 shields

Chug Jug

The Chug Jug is kind of new to Fortnite: Battle Royal. It will give you 100% health and shield. Now, that's great and all, but it takes a full 15 seconds to drink. It's a legendary rarity which means you won't see it often, but you're super lucky if you do because it's extremely powerful.

- Drops in a stack of 1
- Maximum stack is 1
- A chug jug takes 15 seconds to use
- Gives you 100% health and shield
- Legendary rarity

In general, here's how these items rank against each other.

Bandages < Med Kit < Slurp Juice = Small Shield Potion < Shield Potion < Chug Jug

As you can see bandages are the weakest and the most common – so much so that you'll likely use them once you get your hands on them, and the Chug jug is the best, but super rare.

Healing and Shields Tips

- If you're going to use some bandages, use them before you drink any slurp juice. That way you'll hit 75 hp with the bandages and not waste any of the hp you'll get from the slurp juice.

- For you overall health, having bandages on hand isn't a bad idea. If you happen to be an aggressive player that is always fighting then they're your new best friend. You can use them before you pick up medkits - which will fully heal you- from one of those dead bodies and use it immediately.

- If you can use healing items as soon as you get them, then go ahead. It's better to patch yourself up while you're under cover than to be fumbling around while you're in battle.

- Keep in mind you always have campfires! You might have one, but they might not be showing in your inventory because a trap or launch pad is in the way. They're good for an emergency heal or getting to 100 hp if you only have bandages.

- If the storm is coming and you know you'll be in it, grab some of those bandages to survive. Yes, you can actually heal yourself through the storm ONLY if you time it right.

- Depending on which circle you are on, the storm will actually tick for different amounts of damage. It will also increase in damage when it completes, so thoroughly calculate how much heals you will need as well as when to stop and heal up before you continue to run.

- If you can find a slot for it, chug jugs are worth having later on in the game because they give you full health and shields. Only problem is you have to find a good spot to crack it open since it takes 15 seconds to drink.

- You should always carry around small potions. They're easy to gulp down and they will give you 25 shield points with a maximum of 50 at a time. This makes them perfect for when you're fighting.

- If you have to decide between one healing or shield item late into the game, go with the small shield potion and get your healing items from downed enemies.

Weapons in Fortnite: Battle Royale

Sure, you can win a round in Fortnite with nothing but a pistol and a couple of grenades, but only if you're extremely good or very lucky. If you're neither of these, then it would be wise of you to stock up on the best weapons and build the perfect load out that's great for any range.

With this in mind, I'll let you in on some tips that will help you manage you inventory and get familiar with the weapons you should have.

How to Set Up Your Inventory

Balance your loadout

Sure, grabbing the best guns in the game is important, but it's also vital that your collection of weapons is well balanced.

A good weapons collection will give you a gun for every situation, while a bad collection will cause your down fall. For example, you can carry around a Tactical shotgun which is great for close ups, but when you use it at a mid to long range it will certainly fail.

Now, if you ever find yourself lacking a close-range weapon, don't be afraid to drop your shotgun for the weapon you need. Or if you have plenty of shotguns, clear some space for something like a scoped rifle whenever you have the chance. This should be a no-brainer, but a lot of players will continue to stick with the gun that's wrong for the situation they're in.

Depending on how you play Fortnite, your five slot inventory spaces should be filled with these 6 items including the guns I mentioned before:

- An assault rifle or a silenced pistol
- A shotgun
- A sniper rifle

- Explosives (a rocket launcher is preferred)
- Shields
- Healing items

You can take my advice and have four weapons and one set of shields or healing items. When you need to, you can just heal up after killing an enemy and then pick up a shield potion or a med kit from their body, use it and then grab your weapon again.

The Best Weapons For Your Inventory

In this section, I'll break down the best weapons you can get your hands on in Fortnite: Battle Royale. As I said before, you have your foundation and everything else is a luxury.

Anyways, the weapons go by colored rarities. In total there are five different kinds of rarities including:

- Grey - Common
- Green - Uncommon
- Blue - Rare
- Purple - Epic
- Gold - Legendary

If you're not familiar with their tier system, then you should know that the better the rarity the harder it is to get your hands on it. Legendary weapons are also extremely rare, but they're super powerful.

Top 5 Weapons in Fortnite: Battle Royale

Everyone has their favorite guns in Fortnite, so below I'm listing off my personal favorites and why I think they're really good. Just bear in mind that this isn't a stat list in any way, and that different players will be better with some weapons while others will not.

M16 (Assault Rifle)

If you want to have a common drop that's well-rounded when it comes to everything, then the M16 is worth hunting down. It comes in handy in a short to mid-range exchange, delivers a decent amount of damage and has enough accuracy that it will take down an opponent after a few shots

During long range engagements, the M16 does struggle to make it through because the bullet spread can vary the more you hold the trigger down. To correct this, opt to tap on the trigger lightly, but you still need to be accurate if you want to cause any damage to your target.

Bolt Action/Semi-Auto Sniper Rifle

Having a sniper rifle in your inventory will definitely increase your chance of ending the game victorious. A sniper rifle will eliminate enemies instantly, but you have to perfect your aim as well as take in account the bullet drop and then get a headshot in to do so.

As the matches go on, having a sniper rifle becomes more and more important. When that circle starts getting smaller, you can hold a fixed position with your sniper rifle and quickly spot targets you want to take out without getting too close.

I will say that I do prefer the Bolt Action over the Semi-Auto mainly because you can make every shot count and it just plays better. It will reward your accuracy and you can get into a good position with it.

Pump/Tactical Shotgun

No inventory would be complete without both the Pump and Tactical shotguns. These two are the perfect pair for close-range duels. Even though the Pump has a slower fire rate, if you land a hit it can deal out 95 damage - enough to almost one-shot an opponent! The only way you can really take advantage of this gun is if you have good aim, a missed shot can be downright deadly.

My other favorite is the Tactical Shotgun that has a higher fire rate but less damage. It's a lot easier to handle since it's not super reliant on you making pinpoint accurate shots. So, you're safe to jump around all over the place will being trigger happy.

Rocket Launcher

Strangely enough, the explosive goodness of the Rocket Launcher is a great tool for destroying forts or some of the environment. Of course, you can use it to kill off an entire group of enemies, but it's better to use it here and there as a way to wipe out their cover and leave them wide open.

With this weapon, you also have to remember that ammo for it is pretty scarce, so you'll need to loot plenty of ammo crates to have a decent supply of rockets.

SCAR (Assault Rifle)

At the moment, the SCAR assault rifle is the strongest weapon in the game. It's basically the M16's reliable big bro and it can handle just about anything.

With no unique characteristic or extra design elements, the SCAR just seems like a very standard weapon. But it isn't, it comes with some pretty outstanding accuracy, as well as excellent damage and is surprisingly effective at all ranges – and I really appreciate that.

If you want to get your hands on one, you should know that the SCAR only drops as an Epic or Legendary. So, looting chests or shooting down enemies are your best bet.

Weapon Looting Tips

Here are a few other things you should keep a look out for while you're looting, along with some tips.

- In this game, any gun with a scope is a must! With one in tow you can do some damage from a safe distance – which is a plus in any kind of shooting game. Most of the engagement you have in this game will take place from a medium to far range, so a scope is super useful.

- Keep your supplies high. It would be a shame to run out of sniper bullets when you have the perfect kill in sight.
- This is a no-brainer, but if you come across a weapon that is higher than the rarity of your current weapon, go ahead and swap it out. An instant upgrade on whatever you're carrying is always great.
- On the flip side, don't always drop a weapon that works for you for another one that's rarer. Sometimes it's best for you to hold on to a common assault rifle over having a blue SMG. You just need to account for your own play style before you make the decision to swap.
- Don't brush off those Supply Crates you see dropping from the sky. They're packed with powerful loot, so they're actually worth chasing down and fighting over.

Pro Weapon Tips

Play like a pro by dealing with your weapons like one with these tips below!

Keep the SCAR Close

Why? Because it's one of the best guns, hands down. Thanks to its high damage and accuracy, it will give you a huge advantage when you're fighting –well unless you're fighting with a sniper, but other than that you're sure to walk away victorious.

Oh, I did mention that they're rare, right? Anyways, you might get lucky and get one from a chest at the start of the game. If not, then you might get one from supply drops or another players' dead body.

Always grab an assault rifle and a shotgun at the start

No matter what, try to secure an assault rifle and a shotgun the moment you land on the island. These two are the bare minimum you need to get started, so don't worry about anything else until you have these two in your hands.

If you can't find an assault rifle right away, at the very least you should grab a SMG. You need to have something up front that has a good range and can pack a punch up close. As long as you have this much you can get everything else you need as you go along, either by looting it or killing off opponents.

Switch Between Guns depending on the Location or What Range You're Fighting At

It should really go without saying but starting a fight with the wrong gun is just as bad as not having one at all. That's why you have to switch things up in Battle Royale.

For example, when you enter a house always switch to a shotgun and then when you leave switch back to an assault rifle. This is mainly because in a confined space a shotgun will beat out an assault rifle every time. And the same rule applies to a tactical SMG, which will give you more of an advantage in an open space than a shotgun.

Reorder guns in your inventory

It's really simple and well, essential to reorder your gun inventory. So, when you have a moment to spare, open your pack and move your guns. Ideally, you'll want to place your assault rifle/shotgun combo right next to each other in the front. This will make it easier for you to switch them at a push of a button and it will make a huge difference in those ever changing combat situations.

DPS Beats Damage, Especially If You're a Poor Shot

Like I went over before, Fornite's weapons are set at a specific rarity value, with the order going like this:

- Grey - Common
- Green - Uncommon
- Blue - Rare
- Purple - Epic
- Gold- Legendary

Generally speaking, there are common, uncommon and rare variants for most of the weapon types, but only some include epic and legendary types like sniper rifles and assault rifles.

The higher types will always win because rarer weapons offer more damage. For example, if there was a one-on-one fight between a blue M16 and a Grey M116, the blue one would beat it.

However, when it comes to a battle between different kinds of guns, things aren't really that simple. That's why you have to look at the damage and fire rate which combines to make the DPS to find the best weapons.

Play to your strengths (and weaknesses)

In Fortnite:Battle Royale, you'll eventually notice that the trade-off of high damage weapons is often a very slow fire rate —which is done to probably even out the playing field. For instance, a pump shotgun can instantly kill an enemy with full health and shields all in one shot. But if you miss your shot, then you'll have to wait a few more seconds to fire again. In a close-range battle, these few seconds can feel like ages.

Now, if your aim is pretty bad, then a tactical shotgun would be a better option for you. These deal less damage in a single shot, but it will deliver more damage per second all thanks to its fast fire rate. Meaning you're likely to be more successful and land a few shots.

The same rings true with snipers. Although the bolt-action single shot rifle is better, newbies who are still learning how to aim might fit better with a semi-automatic sniper which will help them get used to bullet drop-off.

As you play you might feel you click better with some weapons than others, and that's great! So feel free to prioritize them the way you want. Some players like the silenced pistol – which does deal less damage, but it's quiet – to an assault rifle. But it basically comes down to how well You perform with the weapon, and what you think about the trade-offs.

Later down the line after you improve in Fortnite and your aim gets better, you'll be choosing those high damage weapons without worrying since you'll miss fewer shots.

Try and Pick a Burst Rifle

Listen, I know you won't like it, but try and grab a three-shot burst rifle if you can. It will make you a better shot, mainly because when you spray your bullets you end up losing accuracy. Plus, at medium to long ranges tighter shooting of a burst rifle will always equal a win.

If you're really worried about the fire rate, then just squeeze the trigger more.

Use the Mini Gun for Destroying Buildings

Mini guns are an absolute beast when it comes to weapons. While they look terrifying, they're not the best thing to bring to a firefight thanks to its slow aim and wide spread.

You can, however use it to destroy end game buildings and protective walls. As a bonus, the spraying of that many bullets will cause panic and damage your opponents the whole time you're firing it.

Save Silenced Weapons for Ambushing Opponents

Weapons like suppressed submachine gun and handguns aren't on the top of many people's must-have list in a firefight, but the silent ones are very useful.

They're quiet and it will make it harder for enemies to find you. In fact, you'll most likely get in a lot of damage before people find you and retaliate. This will give you a clear advantage, especially when two or more people are fighting and you've joined in from afar.

Solo Tips, Tricks and Strategies

Going solo in Fortnite: Battle Royale can be really stressful. It's basically you against the world with no one to help you out when you really need it. Yup, it's all up to you to make the right choices, build a pro structure, get gear quickly and survive every fight.

It isn't easy, but it's not impossible either and it can be fun. Below I'll be sharing with you some tips that will help you bag more solo victories.

- Choose where you land wisely! It will definitely set the tone for the rest of the match. If you go for a very popular area, you'll see a lot more fighting, but will have a greater chance of getting good loot. Picking a more peaceful and quieter spot will increase your chances of survival early, but you do need to look for enemies and plan out your looting if you want to survive late into the game.
- Each time you loot a chest I haven't talked about in this book, try to memorize the location for next time. That way you can get gear as fast as possible in every match.
- Don't forget about ammo boxes! You need to always have a steady supply of ammunition.
- When you're traveling from one destination to the other, or have some down time, keep harvesting materials no matter what.
- Building resources like wood, brick and metal are always needed. Trees, pallets, boulders and cars are all decent supply sources.
- Use the fact that you can build your way to higher ground to your advantage in every fight.
- Stay level headed and calm when you're facing enemies. It's really easy to freak out when you're by yourself, but you need to figure out what you need to do to win any battle.
- If you ever run out of ammo with your primary weapon during a shootout, quickly swap to a second weapon to take them out. Or, you can find some cover and reload really fast - remember that enemies can try and take advantage of you during this time.

- No matter where you are or what you're doing, listen closely for footsteps. It's already difficult enough trying to figure out where the enemy is, but at least if you can hear them coming you can prepare better.

- Decide how you're going to play around the coming Storm before you jump into the game. If you're a beginner player, you can either chase the circle as it closes in and play around the edge. Or you can take the initiative and find a good place before the Storm Cloud comes in. The storm will force people into the area and it will be an advantage for you.

Duo Guide - Tips, Tricks and Strategies

Games are always better with friends, especially Fortnite: Battle Royale. While playing solo is intense, playing this game with a wingman can be a more relaxed and fun experience.

When you're playing solo, it pretty much comes with that 'every man for himself' attitude. But when you play with a friend it's of course different and it relies on good communication when it comes to fighting, building and exploring the environment together for some amazing loot.

Below, I put together a few tips and tricks that will help you and your friend win as a duo in all aspects of the game including combat, building, looting as well as positioning.

Landing with Your Partner

Before you even land, it's important that you talk about what locations you want to target. My advice is to focus on one building, then land and head to the same location together or split up for a while to find separate loot.

As long as you guys land in the same area, you can always call for back up if you're in trouble while you're picking up supplies. So, it's really important that you react quickly while opening chests or when you need to respond if your teammate needs help.

Fighting with Your Partner

The best part of playing with a partner is you have someone who will have your back. So anytime you're in a little bit of trouble or an enemy is approaching – call it out to your partner.

Never be too quiet while playing and talk to them, because communication is vital when you're playing with an ally. Remember while you're fighting that time is precious, so don't be too descriptive when you're talking to them. Keep everything really simple. For example, use the compass and tell them which direction they're heading or describe something interesting nearby.

When you're finally in battle, try and spray down the same opponent to get rid of them faster. Just call out which enemy you want target and go then for it. You can also do this with structures as well.

Of course, you can't prepare for everything, so it's always great to work together with your partner on the fly. But I can tell you that your best bet is to flank instead of having you or your partner sneak around the enemy. You should also get to higher ground by building a structure together to overlook your opponents and take them out.

And finally, always remember that you're a duo so you have to approach every situation as two.

Squad Tips, Tricks and Strategies

Playing Fortnite Battle with a group of friends is a completely different experience. Not only do you have to think about yourself, but you have to think about three other people as well. So it can be hard keeping a group of people alive to the end.

But don't worry, I have some great tips and strategy advice that will help you and your squad emerge in the number one spot.

Squad Tips and Tricks

- Anytime you play in a group, communication is always key. Let your teammates know when you see an enemy near, what direction they're heading and any interesting points that are nearby. Keep things short so you guys don't get confused.

- Make the best of the time you have in the pre-game lobby. Go over where you want to land, if you might stay with another teammate or how you're going to go about playing the match – passively or aggressively.

- When you're traveling from point a to point b, I can't stress enough how important it is to harvest as much building materials as possible.

- Make sure you destroy trees, boulders, cars, pallets or just anything to make sure your squad has a ton of resources. This is one of the best ways to keep materials on you and avoid running out.

- While you're looting, call out what you've picked up and what you left behind. Save your teammates healing items, weapons or ammunition if they need it.

- It's good to stay close to each other but avoid running around in a pack. Instead, keep your distance from one another so you guys don't get shot together at the same time.

- Always look for opportunities to flank other opponents since this throws them off and splits their focus. Teams that are flanked are known to crumble because they don't know where the enemy is or what they're up against.

- When your team is building a structure, only have one or two members doing this to minimize the confusion.

- If you're in the middle of a firefight and a teammate is knocked down, play for yourself first and then go to your teammate when it's safe. Otherwise you leave yourself open to being attack.

- It's good to remember that if you knock down an opponent and they're eliminated while going down, then their entire team is gone as well.

Intermediate and Advanced Fortnite Tips

Change how you play and make it into the top 10 with these intermediate and advance playing tips!

When To Build

Knowing exactly when to build in Fortnite can be confusing, especially for those who just like to play campaigns. Even if you want to build a huge fort, most of the time it isn't practical because the Storm will eventually come and destroy everything. Also, while you're in craft mode it's easy for an enemy sniper to pick you off.

But there are times when building comes in handy, for instance when you're using healing items. Those things can be really slow, so it's a good idea to build a wall around you for cover before you spend a few seconds of downtime to heal.

Throwing up a single panel wall also works as a great barrier in a cramped building. Same goes for when a well armed, high hp opponent is coming your way. For a good laugh, you can toss a grenade over the wall at them if you have one.

Use your building tool as a way to escape too. For example, if you're in a valley where a battle is going on, get to higher ground and avoid the firefight by throwing up three or four wooden stairs panels.

Same goes for when you can't reach a certain area. You can build your own way up all while shielding it with a side or two. This way you can have a cool sniper nest until the storm approaches.

Choosing Landing Points

You should know that jumping straight into a building filled with loot is a great way to die and rank 99 or 100. That's mainly, because anyone who willingly does this are all going to gun each other down shortly after landing.

Now I did cover good places that everyone can land and loot, but I'll add two extra locations to the list that are more suitable for intermediate and advanced players.

Loot Lake

Right in the center of the map is where you'll find Loot Lake. This place is certainly a gamble but let me say it's worth it. There's a house on the lake island that has at least two golden chests, and another golden chest in the boat that sits on the lake.

The only problem with the lake area is the terrain. It's wide open and if you're not fast enough you will certainly die by the hands of other players.

Your best bet is to get to this area first and then run away from it before anyone else comes. But if you see other players dropping from the bus nearby, avoid the lake all together.

Anarchy Acres

The other place that's great for more experienced players is the Anarchy Acres farm area. Its located at the end of the map near the storm's edge. To get there, you'll have to wait to jump out of the battle bus, which is a clear disadvantage if someone else gets there before you. However, most people don't wait, they just drop out of the bus as fast as they can. If you play it differently you'll end up with some crazy good weapons and healing items just by using the "edge of the storm" strategy..

Stay Alive and Play the Game

There's a clear difference between surviving and *winning* in Fortnite. Even though the map is smaller and its constantly shrinking to bring you face to face with your enemies, it's still common for players to get into the top 10 −20 just by hiding. But hiding...is that how you want to get there?

Here are some better ways you can spend your time in the game and make it into the top 10:

- *Scout through heavily scavenged locations* and then kill off anyone who is coming out with new loot. Be sure to be on the lookout when you go in to grab the loot, other players might be playing the same strategy.
- *Go ahead and build a sniper's nest* on top of an existing structure or building. This will give you a clear line so you can pick off anyone who is advancing.
- *Wait around near the edge of the safe zone* and then get ready to take off those players who are rushing in as the storm comes in closer.
- *Be fearless and stay at the edge of the storm.* You should only move when you have to, so you can avoid getting shot from behind.

Regardless of what strategy you use, you will eventually get into a firefight. So, when this happens those really annoying spazztastic motions can work in your favor, especially when the other player is armed with an automatic weapon.

Automatic weapons spray bullets like crazy and they aren't that accurate, so randomly zaggaing from left to right, jumping, crouching and standing up can keep you alive. You can also throw up a wall if you think it will help you escape.

But it's better to not be seen at all, than to be spazzing out. To avoid the latter, stay covered and quietly make your way to your next position.

Sound Cues

I can't stress enough how important it is to play Fortnite Battle Royale with a set of quality headphones. Sound plays such a huge role in the game, and you're just putting yourself at a disadvantage if you don't.

With your headphones on you can hear every movement – especially Loud sprinting – from faraway. These sounds will let you know that someone has seen you and they're coming to kill you off. If you're lucky, it might just be an inexperienced player who is sprinting through the open begging to be shot – yeah, don't be that guy.

Firing a weapon can also be super loud in Battle Royale, and you can actually track it back to its original location through sound if there's no battle going on.

Another thing that has a loud sound are golden chests, and their sound is pretty distinct.

Land Faster

If you're not looking to go the peaceful and quiet route, then get to land faster. You've probably seen plenty of other players getting lower than you and landing before you even get out of the bus.

You can do this by pulling your glider out at a certain height based on what's right below you. So just look for the lowest point on the map and head over to it. Once you've pulled your glider out you can better assess where you can and can't land. It does take a bit of practice to get a sense of when you should exit the battle bus and how far you can reach.

Scout Around for Enemies

While you're gliding to your potential landing spot, don't forget to look around and make a note of where your opponents are landing. Doing so will give you a sense of what you're about to go up against and if you need to grab your gun quickly.

For instance, if someone happens to land in the same building or house as you, then you'll know from the start you need to get a gun. When you find a decent one, you can then go in for the kill to prevent them from advancing. Plus, getting frags on unarmed opponents is a really easy way to get kills.

But if it's possible, try really hard to avoid landing in the same building or area as another player, because sometimes it doesn't work out in your favor. They might get the gun first or they could start hacking away at you with their pickaxe.

If you land fast and get your hands on a decent mid to long distance gun immediately, then go ahead and use it to get a few easy kills in. Just position yourself well and start taking shots at people who are still getting themselves together or hacking into buildings or houses.

Loot Quickly

One thing I've noticed is that a lot of new players take their time getting loot. In this kind of game you need to get look quick, so you have no choice but to cover a lot of land and then move on to the next area.

You'll also need to have a plan in mind that includes what kind of gun you want and what slots you want them in. Also, you don't have to worry about getting small ammunition if you're not going to carry a run that uses it.

Loot Thoroughly

Don't leave good loot behind! Unless you have to move from the areas really fast, make sure you get your hands on every piece of loot there. Check every chest spot and go through every house that hasn't been looted. You know in this game you'll need lots of loot, plus every chest is a chance to improve your weapon inventory and gain more shields and healing items.

Know Where the Chests Are At

It's all about location and a bit of experience when you're searching for loot. I've mentioned a couple of areas that have chest spawns in a different section, but overall you have to learn these locations for yourself. You should also make it a point to land in different looting spots too.

Always Gather Resources and Don't Break the Trees

While you run from one location to the other, take you pickaxe out and hack away at the trees and wooden palettes (these supply a decent amount of wood and can be found in buildings as well as other area).

I highly recommend that you do this until you have at least 500+ wood in stock. You really won't be able to keep it around as you advance on other players.

If you want to make it through as low-key as possible then don't break the trees all the way. It will only allow other opponents to spot you from a distance since the animation of a tree falling is so noticeable.

So just hack the tree down to the last hit, stop and then move on without destroying it.

Extra Resource Tips

- Ever notice that small circle when you are harvesting something? Well, if you aim at that button on your next strike with your harvest tool you'll be able to get resources like tress, walls and boulders much faster.
- Get enough resources from a ramp or two early on in the game. This will give you a huge advantage over players who only have limited loot and no resources. You'll be able to easily win a fight in a few minutes just because you can build a ramp.
- Harvest bricks by mining various boulders that are all over the map. It's similar to how trees are the best for wood, but these will give you a decent amount of brick.

Don't Harvest Walls for Resources

Unless you're really desperate, don't harvest resources from houses or furniture. The fastest way to get them is from harvesting trees, wooden pallets and stone boulders, If you're in need of metal, go crazy on a couple of cars and any other metal objects.

Take Advantage of the 3rd Person View

When you're in a building or behind a wall, and an opponent is hanging around, hug up next to the wall and take a look around the corner/door via third person view. It will allow you to find your opponent so that you can kill them off. Once you have their exact location, you need to sidestep out enough to fire and then quickly sidestep back while your shotgun* reloads.

*Note that a shotgun is usually the best weapon to use in this kind of battle.

Equip Your Pickaxe While Looting

Okay, this may sound weird, but when you're going through a pile of loot only equip your pickaxe, so whatever you pickup doesn't swap out with what you're currently carrying. Not doing this could get you into a lot of trouble, especially if you drop your weapon for some bandages and then you suddenly get into a fight.

By doing this, you'll be able to complete stacks of all stackable items without swapping out items like bandages, shield potions, medkits, etc.

It's a great way to make sure you loot faster, and you can also grab all the loot you want. You could even head into the Storm for a short time just to get your hands on a few shields or other quality items like medkits or campfires.

Always Be Moving

No matter how many times I play, I'm always shaking my head when I see players who just stop moving. Don't ever be that player! You'll end up listening to the music in the lobby next all thanks to a sniper's bullet.

So unless you're throughly protected from every single side, never stop moving. Make things hard for people, drink a potion or use a medkit and move from side to side. Most importantly, while you're in a fort never peak your head out to look at nothing. More often than not, you'll be eating another player's bullets soon.

Shoot Those Supply Crates and Drops

Want a lot of good loot? Then look for some supply crates and keep track of them by shooting at it once.

When you do this, you'll then see a HP bar that is visible through walls or mountains. With it, you'll be able to see if the crate has been opened which gives you a chance to take out any nearby players. If you have a lot of ammo you can just take it down yourself, but only if you know for a fact that it's safe to do so.

Be Aware of the Storm

One of the easiest ways to get killed in Fortnite isn't from a snipers bullet, it's from forgetting about the storm until it's too late. So here's exactly what you need to know about it.

For starters, the first and second storm will move in fast, but they are traveling from faraway, so it will take a while for them to come close. You won't be able to out run them when they start to get close to you. After those two circles, you can then outrun the circles closing in. Always play it safe on the second circle, for the first one you will usually have enough time to reach the safe zone from most areas.

If you're really far away, then you'll need to avoid fight since a long battle can take up precious time. But then again, if you know you're going to be in the storm and you're low on health, then you might have to risk it and take down a few enemies in the hopes you get healing items.

Now, if you think you may die while getting to the circle, pick up bandages (you can replace another it pen if needed) and/or a medkit and run out of the storm while healing. You're able to keep track of how much damage the storm is doing to you since it ticks every second. So you can in fact calculate how many seconds you can delay before you have to use a bandage or medkit. Remember, bandages take 4 seconds and medkits take 10 seconds to use.

You can also check and see if you have a handy launch pad that's ready to use. Your final option would be to grab some impulse grenades and jump yourself out.

So pay attention, plan your escape and don't give up!

10 Rookie Mistakes You've Been Making In Fortnite: Battle Royale

Now you've been playing Fortnite: Battle Royale for a while without any wins. But why? It could be because you're making a bunch of rookie mistakes that are holding you back

Thankfully, these mistakes are easy to avoid if you take my advice. These tips won't transform the way you play over night, but they'll definitely help you ditch that rookie mindset. So next time You'll play smarter and hopefully get to that coveted top spot.

You're Lacking in Confidence

Things can get so stressful when you realize you're on an island with 99 other people who all want to kill each other. Heading for safety in the bushes or an abandoned structure can be really tempting, Plus, even if when you move as the storm shrinks the battlefield, it's easy for these same players to sneak into the top 10 by just staying out of sight and avoiding any game ending conflicts.

Now, it's a huge mistake to play so defensively. Even if you become one of the last players standing without firing your gun, you still have to kill someone to take that top spot. And to be in that top spot, you have to confidently know your stuff! I mean you can only learn so much from reading, you have to get out there and actually play.

I'm not saying you should be reckless, like rushing into the middle of a firefight. Instead, you need to observe and pick your shots carefully, but don't shy too much away from it. To get even better, gain some much-needed confidence by practicing if you want to take out other skilled players.

As you practice you might lose – a lot, but you'll get better over time. Feel free to exit out of an on-going game after you die since there's absolutely no penalty for that.

Even if you lose, you can be back in the game in just a few seconds. So, practice, gain confidence and kick some butt.

You're forgetting what makes Fortnite Unique

You may be wondering, what makes Fortnite unique? Building and crafting is what makes Battle Royale different from PlayerUnknown's Battlegrounds. It's actually a crucial part of the game, mostly at the end of a round and you'll need to master it as soon as possible.

I've gone over what you can build in the crafting section. But here's a few items:

- Panic Walls
- Ramps
- Stairs
- Sniper Nests

Crafting does come with a risk, such as gathering materials which takes time and makes noise, and player-built structures that can be seen on the map (giving away your location, but it's worth it).

You're Pressing All the Wrong Buttons

Collecting weapons and gathering the right gear is only half the battle. You need to have your fingers on the right buttons at all times. Fortnite battles are super quick and they can be brutal, during this time you don't want to be fumbling all over the place for the correct gun to take down your enemies. In order to avoid this, keep the best weapons at your fingers and by keeping the same class of weapons in the same inventory slot whenever you play.

One of the most common pattern is to set it up by weapons range, like this:

- Shotguns
- Assault rifles
- Sniper rifles

In reality the order isn't important, it's all about consistency. You really don't want to stop and think about which button does what when you only have a few seconds to decide in battle.

So, ditch that rookie mindset and reorder your inventory asap!

You're Too High In the Sky

In Fortnite: Battle Royale all players start each match in the same place – the sky. As you may of guessed, you need to pick the right spot on the playing field and get there as fast as you can. During the very beginning of the match, your main focus should be on looting for weapons and getting crafting materials. Grabbing all the goodies in your starting location it will give you an advantage and you'll also be well prepared for any battle that comes your way. You just have to get there before everyone else.

Now, there are a couple of tricks you can use to land faster. For starters, don't open your glider on your own, let it deploy automatically. That way you can free fall for much longer because your glider isn't slowing you down. The second trick is to stay above flat, low elevated terrains like an open field or river. Your glider actually opens based on the height between you and the ground. So If you're falling above a high point like a mountain, then you might open your glider when you don't want to and descend slower. This may cause you to miss out on all the good loot in your area because someone got there first.

Don't allow that to happen! Fall smart and fast.

You're Not Using Your Senses

Rookies in Fortnite only use their eyes while playing. Pros on the other hand listen closely to pick up on a lot of valuable information.

So play like a pro and keep your ears open for footsteps, gunshots and other noises like a pickaxe breaking down trees. The noises that are made by characters are "louder" than many of the other multiplayer shooters, so by the time you hear another player nearby, you'll be able to prep for battle or run away if you're not ready.

Since sound is directional in Fortnite, invest in a good pair of headphones. They don't have to be super fancy to help you hear better. Speaking of hearing better, you should also turn off the in-game music too, it will allow you to hear other important sound effects while you play.

Besides other characters' noises, you can also hear Treasures chests and safes- which holds the best loot- make a special sound when you're nearby. Some players say it sounds like a heavenly choir, so when you hear it or something like it, start looking for the loot.

And remember that chests are sometimes behind hidden walls or other objects.

Also, be mindful of the noise around your body IRL. Sometimes your headset can pick up background noise – like that playlist you're blasting while you play – and it can make it into the in-game. Don't let this happen to you, but if you hear it from another player use it to your advantage.

You're Lousy at Gathering Resources

As soon as possible, start stocking up on crafting materials. It becomes really hard to do so when the map gets smaller and you have enemies breathing down your neck. And you never want to run out of materials as your building a tower or when you're in the middle of a firefight.

So be sure to pick up your pickaxe and start swinging like a pro - which is something that most don't know how to do, but I'll fill you in here.

When you're using a pickaxe, you'll soon see a blue circle appear on the target. As you hit it, you will deliver more damage to the structure. Hitting the target will even allow you to cut down trees, rocks and walls in half the time. This is a huge advantage when you're trying to get materials faster and it will also help you get to those hidden chests before your opponents.

Some players- including myself, highly recommend that you leave the trees with some health since the stumps can act like a trail of bread crumbs that will lead other players to you. This is easy to do, just stop swinging your axe before the tree is fully looted. There are pros and cons to this strategy since you're stopping yourself from looting all the wood. So if you find that having more wood is better for you at the moment, then chop down the whole tree and quickly, but quietly move on.

You're standing a little too Much

You can't crawl through bushes in Fortnite: Battle Royale like you can in PlayerUnknown's Battlegrounds, but you can crouch. So use this function! It will not only make you smaller, it will help you blend in with the bushes and make your weapons way more accurate -especially if you're using an assault rifle.

You're Not That Accurate

Let's talk about accuracy for a moment. Right now, Fortnite has a system in place known as "bullet spread" or "bloom." This means where you aim is the only factor in whether your shot hits its target or not. There is also a little "random" element thrown in there too. SO, your bullets will only hit inside the crosshairs, they won't fire straight down the middle. Bullet spread will allow bullets to hit the edges of the circle, the center or somewhere in-between.

However, the Bloom effect is aggressive and will often lead to missed shots. There's only a couple things you can do to get around this. One being you can crouch - which shrinks the size of the crosshairs and reduces the bloom - and the other would be to stay still or pause between shots. Use what you know about the system and one of these three positions to better your shot.

You're Not Utilizing Materials correctly

In Fortnite, there are three main types of crafting materials you can have: brick, wood and steel. But did you know that each material has three different statistics that are all related to how strong the materials is.

When you start building a structure out of any material, it will then be given an amount of health or hp (hit points). As you continue to play, the structure will gain health until it reaches a maximum hp that is related to the material.

Wood structures have really good health from the start and they grow fast, but they also have the lowest maximum health. Steel on the other hand is weaker than wood at first and takes much longer to grow, but overall it has the most health. Bricks are somewhere in-between since they do gain health at the same rate as steel, but has more hit points that shell and less hit points than wood. It's overall max health is somewhere in the middle.

These facts will definitely help you in the game. You can use wood if you need to drop a wall in front of oncoming enemies, but it fails when you need durability. Steel is just right for building really tall towers and bases, but you should never use it to deflect bullets in the middle of a battle. And lastly, brick isn't that great for either of these situations, but it can serve as a backup for steel and it's more common.

Visibility comes into play here too. Wooden walls will definitely leave you open thanks to large gaps, while steel is very hard to see through. So when you're trying to hide, by all means go with steel.

You Need to Study Chest Areas More

Surprise! The worst-kept secret in Fortnite: Battle Royale is: chests don't spawn randomly. At first it may of seem that way, but nope. Fortnite: Battle Royale's map has a limited number of chest spawn locations and while every match can have less chests than spawn points, you'll only see chests in predefined locations.

At first, you probably didn't worry about it much because you were too busying learning how to shoot, craft stuff and what-not. But once you know how to play, know where loot and the best way to get there just by pulling up the map is essential. You need to memorize a few chest locations, along with the best spots to gather materials and what places to avoid - mainly just popular places.

The point of studying is to burn a few reliable routes into your memory so you can get off to an amazing start. Plus, your knowledge of the map will lead you to better loot and victory.

You're Not Robbing Corpses Right

It's pretty clear that you can get loot and other supplies from treasure chests and destroying stuff, but one of the best ways to pick up resources and other consumables like bandages and medkits, along with better weapons is from ransacking the bodies of defeated enemies. Sounds harsh, but this is a battle after all.

To get away with some good loot, you have to be careful about it. For instance, firefights are super noisy and they attract a lot of attention so you never really know whose watching until it's too late. Even though getting those kills is fun, don't run right over to the corpse to take all the loot just yet. Looting bodies like that will leave you vulnerable, and savvier players sometimes camp around during the battle and then pick you off when you go to grab the goods. So be patient and hold off for a few minutes, or if you're feeling really confident you can wait there and use the corpse as bait which means more loot for you.

Remember what I said about equipping your pickaxe? You need to make sure you do this while looting corpses if your inventory is full or you don't want to accidentally drop one of your favorite guns and replace it with something weak.

Plus, you can't drop that pickaxe, so carry it while you gather much needed ammo, some stackable medkits, crafting supplies and other items. And if they have a better gun, what are you waiting for? Pick that up too.

Conclusion

Now, this concludes my Fortnite: Battle Royale Tips, Tricks and Strategies book that will turn any player into a pro! You currently know all things that will name you the winner including how to build faster, what to fill your inventory with, where to loot and so much more.

I'll go ahead and wrap this book up with some vital Do's and Don'ts you'll need to ALWAYS remember before you jump out that Battle Bus.

Do's

FALL HARD AND FAST

Want to get there faster? Then after you take that big leap, press and aim forward. Of course, when you do this your main goal will be to get to any area as soon as possible. That way you'll have first dibs on everything from weapons to ammo and treasure chests.

As you fall, make sure you quickly glance around to see where the other players are landing. If they've landed in your general location then avoid them by aiming away.

CLOSE THE DOOR BEHIND YOU

I mentioned this quickly before, but it's worth mentioning again. An open door usually means one thing in Fortnite's Battle Royale, which is that someone is inside or was inside the building. This will alert you or enemies to potential danger.

So to avoid giving yourself away to early on the game, close the door behind you.

SET DOWN TRAPS

Oh, the traps in Fortnite certainly do take on a whole new meaning in Battle Royale. They can give you some really easy kills, but only if they're set down in the right spot.

You should definitely try placing them near a door or glowing loot since some players run around so fast that they'll have no chance of spotting the trap and fall right in.

Also, Leave THE DOOR OPEN

I did say leaving the door open was pretty much ill advised, but keeping it open is also a good way to lure in a kill hungry player into a death trap. To do this all you need to do is open the door, then find an obscure place, either inside the building or outside in the bushes, and go on to kill whoever comes by.

REMEMBER IT'S ABOUT SURVIVAL

Remember that Battle Royale is all about being the last player standing. So even though it's easy to get all caught up in trying to have the most kills, it would be wise to save your ammo, health and mental energy for the last match.

PRACTICE YOUR SHOOTING

Before you set foot onto the map, start off in the pre-deployment area. This area is where you'll find weapons so you can practice your shooting skills as well as aiming, reloading and switching weapons.

LISTEN CLOSELY

Did you hear that? If you didn't it will seriously cost you. So when you're going inside a building or exploring outside, listen for footsteps, guns reloading, resources being harvested, doors opening and closing, shooting and explosions. All these sounds can give you an advantage in a kill or let you know what areas you need to avoid.

ADJUST YOUR SETTINGS

As you're waiting around for the Battle Bus to take off, don't let those minutes go to waste. Instead, access your settings and adjust them so that they suit your unique play style. While some players like to play with a higher sensitivity, other often turn off the grass, change the game's texture, or remap their controls.

FIND COVER IMMEDIATELY

When you land, hurry up and get moving to the nearest building to avoid being spotted by any potential enemies. Doing so will also give you a chance to prepare for battle as you search for weapons, ammo and other helpful resources.

Don'ts

Walk into OPEN SPACES

In Fortnite, it's best that you don't run out in the open for any reason. Instead, crouch and use trees, buildings, bushes and even cars as cover whenever possible.

If you do have to run through an open space, run zigzag so a sniper can't easily pick you off.

DON'T BUST YOUR GUN FOR FUN

When you get a new gun or explosive in your hands, by all means resist the urge to shoot or blow up something for fun! You'll just make a lot of loud noise and draw some unwanted attention.

AVOID THE STORM

You can survive by alternating between staying in the eye of the storm and finding cover inside a building. But don't wait around too long before you move. Most of the time you can't outrun it and once you're in it, you're chances of survival are lowered.

Don't land at popular SITES

Once the Battle Bus takes off, you can then jump off and parachute to any location on the map. But before you jump, look for areas on the map that other players aren't going to. This way you can avoid being killed early on in the match.

If you want to head to a popular area to pick some players off, land near the location, grab some gear and then sneak over like I've mentioned in the Best Locations to Loot chapter.

Don't Forget to STOCK UP ON SHIELD POTIONS

Healing is great and all, but Shield Potions will keep you alive. They give you some protection and seriously help you when you're shooting it out with another player.

Good luck!

CPSIA information can be obtained
at www.ICGtesting.com
Printed in the USA
LVHW100826021219
639121LV00012B/561/P